I Have Come a Long Way: A Memoir of Immigration

By Patricia Eyamba

Published by NextGen Story: Custom Publishing.

www.nextgenstory.com

To Suguren (God) for his faithfulness;

To Valour for being my son and checking how far I have gone with my writing;

To Francis, my husband, for his moral support;

To my One Sky family: Jennifer Castleden, Kristin Patten, Kelly Chapman, Mike Simpson, and Tawo, for setting the stage for this journey.

To Mali, who never gave up on me; and Dorin who was my go-to person.

To my writing cohort, for giving me the drive and empowering environment.

"I was once afraid of people saying, 'who does she think she is?'
Now I have the courage to stand and say 'This is who I am'"

Oprah Winfrey

"Kind words can be short and easy to speak, but their echoes
are truly endless"

Mother Teresa (1910-1997)

Table of Contents

PART 4 | How I Deal With Adversity

Introduction

Beginnings. I am an immigrant to Canada and some days I still feel like a newcomer. Maybe you've been here a month. Perhaps you've been here ten years. But you still feel like an outsider—alone, frustrated, and more than a little frightened. This is a common thread that is woven into our innumerable experiences as new immigrants, woven in as we carry on with our lives in this vast and often confusing country. I'm just like you.

My name is Eke-Egan Obashi, but my friends call me Eke. Nearly ten years ago my family and I made the huge decision to leave our home in Nigeria and make the move to Canada; this is my immigration story—a story of my personal struggles, vulnerability, trauma, hardship, dealings with loneliness, challenges, successes, achievements, and Faith. It is about my journey as a black Nigerian woman and the lessons that I learned through my experiences. It's about how these lessons are preparing me to face surprises and to pursue my own dreams in a positive way. Ultimately, that is my goal. I am still on this journey because learning is new every day.

My journey started on October 7, 2013, when my husband, our son, and I landed in Winnipeg. As is true for all immigrants, there was a story behind our journey. I am often asked by people in my social circles, "Why did you move to Canada?" I moved because I wanted to provide my son with a different worldview, a pluralistic perspective on life. We had a good life in our homeland: simple but good. We never dreamed of leaving our country, Nigeria, but we were persuaded to move to Canada. Later in my book you'll learn why I say "persuaded."

Your reasons for immigrating may be different from mine, but really that doesn't matter. Maybe you came as a refugee, maybe you came for a better life. Regardless of the reason, we all migrated and left our home countries looking for opportunities that were different from the ones that we left behind.

In writing this book, I allowed myself the space to grow as a "human becoming." I took the time to reflect on my personal biases about white and black people and on the newcomer community in general. My journey has challenged my identity, personal awareness, and previous knowledge, and my story has demonstrated the power of self-determination, resilience, faith, spirituality, community, and strategic positioning.

I am writing about my experiences so that I may bring hope to new and settled immigrants alike. I almost gave up on my dreams because the reality in Canada didn't look one bit like the picture I had in my mind. In this journey of mine, I found myself experiencing mental breakdown, voicelessness, numbness, and confusion—but I have held onto my dreams.

I am an English speaker and highly educated. I was an experienced development practice professional in my home country. Why then did I experience challenges in Canada? That is why I am writing my story. It shows that I needed more than my profile to succeed in my new country; it gives a peep into my experiences; it serves as a form of healing for me from all the accumulated pain caused by the unexpected negative immigration experiences; it allows me to release myself from my secret biases and anger so that I can move on in a better way. It is also to aid future immigrants, so that they will know that things aren't always as simple as they appear to be, although this is not a solutions book.

I am very spiritually minded, so my writing is based on my strong spiritual convictions. When I say spiritual, I don't mean religious. I mean souls that are being transformed and working toward higher emotions. I recognise that I am created free. I choose to walk in that freedom. For me, Life is spiritual and therein lies liberty and freedom.

I realise that my story may not fit comfortably into everyone's box and that's not a problem because I am not writing a solutions book; there are no tips or suggestions on how to immigrate to and settle in Canada. I am only sharing my experiences, which may or may not be relevant to you. However, the fact that this book is in your hands right now does mean a lot to me—I encourage you to take a chance and glance through it; it may be useful in some little ways that count.

Throughout this book, I have used traditional Indigenous names for myself and my family members, as a way of acknowledging our strong Nigerian identity. I have also changed the names of some people in the story to protect their privacy.

Please follow me as I start my life in Winnipeg as a new and settling immigrant, come along as I go through complex experiences, and see how things unfold for me in my new home. As I journey through, one truth keeps re-echoing in my soul, "Only believe and don't give up on your dreams."

Sharing my story has ignited anew my faith, hope, and confidence. Writing this book has helped me to more clearly recognize and deeply value the differences and diversity that we have in Canada, which in turn has reminded me of the beauty of those very differences. I have also obtained a greater understanding of why people do not value these differences at times and make side comments that are negative, why some people can gang up against an innocent person, and why some people just hate and coat it with racism and passive aggression. I now have an increased awareness of my own biases, and I have a greater understanding of the impact of my actions and of how all this knowledge has affected my well-being. A sense of clarity now enables me to be a better human, doing to others what I wish them to do unto me. So, the journey begins.

Chaotic Lagos Traffic. Photo credit: Aaron May

PART 1 | The Invitation

The Invitation

Lagos, Nigeria. It was 5:00 a.m. on a Monday in July of 2012 and I was waking up. That was my normal wake up time. It was so hard to rise from the bed, even with the sudden piercing irritation of my bedside alarm. This day was no different. I then woke Edibenwang, my seven-year-old son, so he could start getting prepared for the day while I rustled up his breakfast and lunch pack. (Edibenwang is the name that my grandmother called my son before she passed; it means Great child in the Ikun language that is spoken where I come from. In Nigeria, names have meanings; they are a kind of prophesying about your child and also a wish for what you want your child to become. Another of my child's names is Abasi-akan Ekong—meaning God has given victory; this is in the Efik language, spoken where my husband comes from. For this book I will use Edibenwang.)

The boiling whistle from the kettle coincided with the barking of my neighbors' dogs to jar me out of dreamland. I had dozed off as I sat in the kitchen waiting to give Edibenwang his bowl of cereal. Just as I was finishing with the breakfast preparations, my husband, Asuqwuo came down to take charge so I could go get ready. This was our daily work and school routine from Monday through Friday.

One good thing about our weekdays was that it was easy for Edibenwang to ride with us in the morning since his school was on our route. Another good thing was that we were spared the hard part of navigating the Lagos traffic to pick him up after school. We would still be at work when his school closed, so sometimes our driver, Tony, would go pick him up from school, or my husband, who owned his own business, would use his lunch time to pick him up. But most especially, we really enjoyed our son's company as we rode along. Those were the moments when his young inquisitive mind would always strike us, as he always asked questions about the sights and sounds that assailed him.

I wish I could erase from his mind what he saw that particular Monday morning in July, but I know that is impossible. Since his father kept providing answers to his questions that just kept coming, I knew this meant that the incident would be engraved in our son's mind. Our child has a special gift for deep reflection. He never accepts anything on the surface. No matter how simple something appears, he has a way of revisiting issues. Yes, my child is different: he is a keen thinker. He likes asking very deep questions, especially the "but why's." He is curious and analytical and always wants to know why green is green and not white.

We had gotten to the Opebi–Salvation bus stop and were now caught in the normal slow traffic caused by the numerous buses angling for space and passengers. Just ahead of us, a bus had pulled into the stop and we saw the usual combined efforts of the Federal Road Safety Corp and officers of the Nigerian police as they battled to ensure traffic flow. Indeed, if not for their efforts, the bus stop would have been turned into a snail's pace traffic jam. While it is difficult to pinpoint what it was that actually happened that morning, it was clear that a policeman was in a scuffle with a bus conductor. (Conductor is the name for someone who directs passengers to the bus.) Soon, another policeman appeared and started raining slaps on the conductor.

The bus driver soon jumped out and attempted to break up the altercation, or at least to stop the officers from beating his ward. By this time the traffic was at a total standstill, as the bus had its doors wide open and was without a driver.

Another policeman soon joined in the beating fest. Both the driver and his conductor were quickly overwhelmed, and they were now sitting on the macadam (broken stone of even size used for surfacing roads and paths) begging for the beatings to stop.

"Why are the policemen beating them, Father? Should policemen be beating people or protecting them? Is it because the bus stopped on the road?" Edibenwang just kept asking questions.

His father finally found his voice. "Yes, policemen should protect us. Even when we do wrong, they are not supposed to beat us, but arrest us."

"Then why are they beating them?" Edibenwang asked again.

But now—as quickly as they had begun—the beatings stopped.

"I'm sure they realized they were acting wrongly—that is why they stopped. I am sure the policemen will be cautioned by their bosses," Asuqwuo replied.

"Is cautioned the same as punish?" Edibenwang asked.

"Yes, it is," his father replied.

At last the traffic moved, and as we drove on Asuqwuo tactfully changed the subject of the conversation. I knew it wouldn't end there, I knew our son who is insatiably curious would bring up the topic again, he would ask why there is violence on the street, he would ask if this is what happens in other parts of the world, he would ask what would have been done differently if it was not Nigeria, and even ask if this could happen to him someday, wondering how he could prevent it. That is the personality of my little guy.

Soon Edibenwang was at school and I was at work; my husband had started work at his business. At the end of that day, we would be together again.

I normally get home before my husband; once he returned from work we would exchange normal pleasantries, fill each other in on our days, and skillfully discuss other issues that we deemed to be important. That evening, we had barely started to relax when the doorbell rang. Edibenwang was in his room, so it was left to me to answer the door.

"Are you expecting anyone?" my husband asked. He quickly added that I should be careful to identify the caller before opening the door. Even though it was just past 7:00 p.m., Lagos drama "full ground," as was said in Nigerian parlance. Anything could happen without warning. In Lagos, security could be an issue sometime even though we live in a relatively safe area with good security system, still, we have to be careful and be sure of who is at our door before we open. Regardless of the time of the day.

Looking through the peephole, I could not believe my eyes. Something remarkable was happening. I was already screaming his name as I opened the door. "Edwatoooo! What are you doing here?" I exclaimed as I let him in. He smiled as he walked over to say hello to my husband. "Edwatooo!" I blurted out again while offering him a seat. I asked what his unannounced mission to our house meant. My husband offered him food, but he politely declined.

Edwat was a young man who, ten years earlier, had walked into my office at One Sky Canadian Institute of Sustainable Living, an environmental NGO in Calabar, Cross River State, Nigeria. (Before living in Lagos, our family had lived in Calabar.) This had been during his university days in Nigeria, and he had come to our office seeking an opportunity as an intern. We already had several Canadian graduate students who were in the organization for the same purpose. He successfully joined the internship program. After he completed his internship, he had been hired as a logistics officer. Along the way he got married to one of the Canadian girls who was also an intern. After their marriage, Edwat relocated to Canada in October of 2007, and my husband and I had only seen him once in the last five years, though we were communicating via email. We were super excited to see him here now.

Edwat settled into a chair and tried to give me the brown envelope that he had been clutching since he first arrived. But I pointed toward Asukwuo, who had just gone into another room. Edwat brought the envelope over to him and started explaining what the contents were.

"I want you guys to fill in these forms; I want you in Canada. Fill out the forms and I will take them back with me when I return to Canada in four days. Aunty, I have sent these forms via email to you several times—but you have not responded—so I have decided to bring them with me so that we can fill in this application together and I am dead serious," Edwat said.

I heard my husband giggling from the other room. And I laughed too. "Edwat how do you expect me to go and start all over in a new country at my age? My career, my husband's business, my relationships and family—what happens to them? That is why I never bothered to respond to your emails," I said.

"This relocation is not for you but for your son. Your life has been spent," was his candid response, forgetting that this is not how you talk to your elders in Nigeria.

His words took us aback. My husband and I immediately looked at each other as the statement hit home. It was hard to take, especially as my husband and I had spent virtually every day planning for Edibenwang and his future.

Edwat left after supper, promising to come back the next day, Tuesday. Asukwuo and I had a lot to consider that evening. My husband's business, Peniels and Valtrif, was gradually becoming a household name. The former was an ice cream and coffee shop with Nigerian cuisine and the latter a house finishing and tile business. Also, due to my background in development, my network had expanded, and I was beginning to get offers from major development agencies. This surprise invitation gave us a chance to carefully evaluate our family's future and then make the necessary decision that would move us forward.

The Decision

Life in Nigeria was very beautiful for our family: we were comfortable enough such that we could afford to travel on our vacations, we had firm Christian ethics, we were blessed with sound mental health, and there was never a dull moment in our lives. Thoughts cascaded down on me: "How can we lose all this and move to a new country when we're not even sure if we can maintain our standard of living in our home country?" These were some of the factors that Asuqwuo and I considered as we pondered Edwat's offer.

Every country has its challenges. Nigeria has her own. One of the most serious is traffic, especially in the capital of Lagos, where we were now living. Lagos is a mixed bag: you must be awake by 4:00 a.m. to beat the traffic if you are working on the Island, but sometimes the hustle and bustle can be fun. You can get almost all of your shopping done while you're sitting in traffic on your way home. Vendors come to your car window with their goods, so you get to shop on wheels. That was what we enjoyed. The noise, excitement, and the craziness pretty much summed up what our Lagos was like. Isn't that why we loved it? That last part elicited a smile.

In contrast to our hesitations, Edibenwang was super excited. His first reaction was, "Yesss!" We probed to find out why he was so excited about the opportunity. He said, "I will not have the Lagos traffic. I will go to school without holdups."

"How about your friends?" I asked.

"I will make new friends and will see my old friends whenever I am visiting Nigeria," he said. "I want to experience schooling and living in Canada. I would like to know what it feels like," he concluded.

Edibenwang had been familiar with Canadians his whole life; even before we moved to Lagos, I had been working with Canadians in Nigeria at One Sky. He had literally been welcomed by Canadians because my Canadian coworkers and the interns had all flooded the hospital when he was born. When he was three, Edibenwang would regularly refer to himself as a Canadian. He frequently fantasized using what I recognized to be a strong imagination. He would say that he was hiking with Aunty Kelly (a Canadian colleague) in Canada. It was crystal clear that he really liked the idea of migrating to Canada. That was a hefty relief to Asuquwo and me. Children see things differently, and Edibenwang was thinking about his freedom. He was looking forward to schooling outside the country. He was happy.

Asuqwuo and I had a sleepless night thinking about Edwat's proposal. The thought of suddenly walking away from the comfort and security we had kept me awake. At one point I heard my husband saying out loud, "Abandoning all we have built for years because of Canada? Nooo!"

The next morning, Tuesday, Edwat came back, and he was unrelenting. After a sumptuous breakfast, he again weighed in. "Canada is a very good country. You have endless opportunities. The school system in Canada is top notch," he continued.

He sure knew how to hit the soft spots, and he knew that Edibenwang was the soft spot when it came to both my husband and me.

At the time, Edibenwang was attending the Avi-Cenna International School in Ikeja, Nigeria. It was a very distinctive school noted for the sound quality of its education. Even though it was fairly expensive, that wasn't a problem.

"Uncle, I know it is not easy uprooting oneself from a known life to an uncertain one. But this uncertainty offers everything positive. It would be positive for your son and would offer you both greater freedom to use your God given talents," Edwat explained to my husband. "Yes, you may not see your relatives as often as you would want to. Yes, you will definitely feel homesick every now and then. But believe me when I say that everything will fall into place once you settle. It will not take you long to settle. I urge you not to throw away this opportunity. I came with the forms. I will fill them out for you. All I need is your information."

It was on this second night that Asuqwuo and I wrote down all the pros and cons of our Canada dilemma. We soon realized that the price to pay was not much. It was our view that while staying in Nigeria had more points in terms of connecting with family and friends, providing Edibenwang with a broader perspective and worldview scored highest.

Even though we were not wholly convinced at this point, we realized that it would be difficult to say no. We reflected on Edwat's earlier words when, talking about Edibenwang, he had emphasized the "endless opportunities to pursue your talent." Canada was an immigrant country with a huge diversity of both people and geography. This would give our son a broad perspective, and he would learn how to be inclusive and to appreciate the beauty of diversity.

It was no surprise, then, that on the third day Asuqwuo

found himself reluctantly providing information as Edwat filled in the forms. We had resolved to go along. It was more like putting our fate in God's hands. We knew that it was beyond us at this point.

Three days after that Edwat took the forms with him to Canada. He travelled via Cross River state to visit his father first.

A few months after Edwat left, we received our first email from the government of Canada acknowledging the receipt of our application. The process then went faster than we had thought. Shortly after, we received another email requesting that we go for our biometrics and medicals. We were on vacation in the United Kingdom when we received the email confirmation of our permanent resident status. We immediately cut short our vacation and returned to Lagos. Days later, Asuquwo travelled to Ghana to get our passports stamped.

Time was a luxury that we didn't have because our international passports were expiring in just a couple of days; we were informed that our visas would also expire along with our passports. The implication was that we would lose provincial nominee status and would then have to start the application process all over again. We had no option but to do our best and travel to Canada within just a few days. This is why we were under serious pressure.

Our time was so limited and we didn't have enough to visit our family who lived in a different state than us. They were one hour away by air, and flights were not very regular; by road they were one full day away because of the deplorable road conditions (similar to what I would later experience travelling to some Indigenous communities in the north end in Winnipeg). Due to time constraints we didn't get to travel to say farewell to our siblings. The best I could do in this situation was to invite my younger brother to come visit us.

That gave me the opportunity to see at least one member of my family. He was the only immediate family member that I was able to see before we left for Canada.

We invested our short remaining time in wrapping up my husband's business, figuring out how to sell our cars, and packing only the needful. I donated most of my belongings to my neighbour because we didn't have the time to be more organized in our packing.

Of course, Edibenwang was beside himself as everything unfolded. You could almost see him walking on air. Canada had become his thought center and he kept asking, "Mama, are we really going to Canada?"

For my husband and me though, there was apprehension about the journey that we had begun. A million questions raised more questions. Our emotions ran from fear to excitement and back to fear in milliseconds.

We tried to arrange a farewell at school for our son, but it never actually happened, and this was disappointing for him. He was only able to say goodbye to his principal and head teacher. Another thing we didn't have time for was shopping for African food and spices, and we left behind most of our clothes because Edwat had told us that we wouldn't need them in Canada. (But we did miss having them and I wish we had brought them—it would have saved us a lot of the money that we spent in our first month in Canada.)

In the pandemonium, we forgot to do what probably would have been the most useful thing of all—researching the country that we were migrating to. We would later feel the tremendous consequences of not finding out more about life in Canada ahead of time.

On the eve of our departure, our pastor's wife Mrs Iderawunmi invited us to their home for dinner. We ate, she prayed for us, and we took pictures of us with her. On the day of our departure the church prayed for us, and our pastor, Mr. Iderawunmi, along with some church members, chauffeured us to the airport to bid us farewell. We deeply appreciated this gesture. It was a good memory that lingered for a long time.

My two cousins also accompanied us to the airport. My cousin Victoria (who was my manager), through her tears, asked if this journey was worth the sacrifice. "Why are you relocating after all the investment?" she asked. She broke down sobbing like a baby. I couldn't resist but joined her as we both hugged and wept on each other's shoulders. It was quite an emotional send off. The prayers from the church gave us strength; they provided us with positive energy.

At the airport we did all of the necessary paperwork and then we were checked in. So, with very little time to prepare, to say our goodbyes to friends and relatives, or to even learn about our new country, our family finally arrived in Winnipeg on October 7, 2013.

We did not know then that we were starting a new journey where faith and hope would kiss each other—a journey of dying and being resurrected in order to make it to heaven. The Holy Book tells us that heaven contains only spirits; it is a place where people of the flesh have already been transformed. This transition makes a huge difference as heaven was made for spirits and the Earth was created for people. In this situation, metaphorically, Canada would become our heaven and we would not die a physical death, but rather some of our perceptions and ideas would have to die so that new ones could sprout. This was going to be our biggest challenge. We had to take in the newness of our location and find the best way to settle in.

PART 2 | Our Arrival

Our Arrival

The first people we met on arrival were warm and welcoming. As soon as my family and I entered the immigration area of the airport, the immigration officer said to us with a beautiful smile, "Welcome to Canada." That made us feel very welcome. The airport was brightly lit and the warm smile of the immigration officer was contagious—but the smile didn't make me forget that I was in a new country.

I will never forget the icy hug that I received from the weather. It was the fall season and it felt really cold to me. I was coming from Nigeria, a tropical country with temperatures around 30°C, to Winnipeg during the fall. The jacket I wore that day was not thick enough to provide warmth. Even in the airport I felt the piercing cold. The immigration officer caught me shivering and jokingly said, "This is the fall season, wait till the real winter arrives." I didn't understand his joke until later in the year. As my family and I were shuffled from one officer's desk to another, I felt my heart begin to race with fear. The reality of our immigration had suddenly hit me in the face. It was a journey that would change my life forever.

We were picked up by Edwat after all of our airport checks were done with. He had stayed in Winnipeg so that he could spend a couple of days helping us. He had arranged for his apartment to serve as a transitional home for us and he was also going to help us with the basic things that we needed to start our new life, one of which was getting the proper government documentation. Edwat had only three days to spend with us before he returned to Nigeria to continue with his new job. Because there was so little time, he wanted to spend every possible moment of it giving us information. He also wanted to make sure that he was able to cover the basic steps with us before he left. Settling into a new country can be a struggle if you don't have anyone to walk you through each new thing. This was my experience in Canada, regardless of the fact that I spoke English. I still needed help with navigating the system. It was new to me and totally different from Nigeria's. The system was very structured and there was a process for everything.

As we were driving to Edwat's home that first night, he unveiled the plan for the next day. He said it was going to be very busy.

We finally arrived at his apartment. I was exhausted and immediately crashed on the floor without waiting for the bed; I was half sleeping and half eating the panini we had bought from Tim Hortons on our way from the airport. My son and my husband were not as tired as I was. I left them sitting at the dining room table while I lay on the floor and dosed off. They, full of energy, continued chatting and watching TV.

The next day Edwat took us to our scheduled visits at various government agencies. The first was to get criminal record checks and child abuse registry checks done, and the second was to start the process of obtaining our social insurance numbers (SIN) through Service Canada. Edwat explained that a SIN was essential for connecting us to most available programs and resources, and it was also needed so that we could work and receive government benefits.

The following day, we focused on getting Edibenwang

registered in school. In the morning, Edwat gave us a ride to the school that he proposed—a private Christian school located in the Fort Garry area of Winnipeg. As we were travelling from the St. James area to Pembina Highway, it gave us the opportunity to appreciate the beauty of the city. It was the fall season, when leaves fall from trees, and the sky was exceptionally clear. The white clouds were so bright, it was as if they were smiling. The sunburnt leaves appearing in red, orange, and brown gave me the feeling of due season, of harvest. It was the season of harvest in Nigeria, when we celebrated the planting seasons. I was focused on admiring the beauty when Edwat pulled over. We had arrived at the school.

We all stepped out of the car and walked into this beautiful school. As we came into the reception area, we were greeted by the administrative secretary and we told her what we had come for. Edwat had called earlier to schedule the appointment, so the school principal and resource teacher were expecting us. The secretary ushered us into the principal's office and the resource teacher joined us. After the get to know you phase, the resource teacher took Edibenwang into her office for assessment. Two hours later they both came out and she said, "Congratulations! He made it through and is qualified to be in grade five. We will give him a chance there but can move him to grade four if we notice he is struggling." (That never happened. He was therefore able to skip a grade as he was nine years old at the time.)

Edibenwang was registered and he was also enrolled in an out-of-school program that was managed by the school. That would give us time to run around while he was in after-school care.

We got through all of Edwat's recommended basic steps within three days. He then returned to Nigeria and we were left all by ourselves. It suddenly dawned on me that I was a sheep without a shepherd. The reality of my vulnerability made me even more confused. The night after seeing Edwat off at the airport we returned home. I sat on the couch thinking of the things that we had to do next and then stood up and walked to the window. Suddenly, I felt a kind of emptiness—as if everything was standing still. It finally dawned on me that I was no longer in Naija! Uncontrollable tears rolled from my eyes as I gazed into space. Fear gripped me. Will I make it here? My son caught me crying, and like he was reading my mind, said to me, "Mama, you are bigger than your fears." Those magic words were like a fire that melted the wax of confusion in my mind. I quickly dried my tears with my hand, turned to him, and gave him a hug. I whispered, "Thank you for your encouraging words."

Edwat's sacrificial three days were something we deeply appreciated. We accomplished so much within the short time that he spent with us, which was really helpful. Within that time my husband was also able to buy a used car. However, it was not insured so Edwat had said that he would lend us his car for the first week following his departure, before he shipped the car out to Nigeria.

Before we went to sleep that night, we developed our to-do list for the next day. I woke up on that fourth day battered by severe cold and more feelings of emptiness. Anxiety and fear of the unknown gripped me like an iron fist. We were now entering into the unknown. We had to accomplish as much as possible within each day. The more we accomplished, the closer we were to settling in.

That first morning of our family being alone in Canada, I quickly fixed breakfast and packed lunch for my son. This was the start of my new weekday routine in my new country, in my new life—a new life and a new house with the attendant to strange happenings that came with them.

Housing Woes

Our true journey started at this point. Because we were all in such a hurry before Edwat had left, he and my husband had only talked briefly about accommodations. Edwat had told my husband how to pay the rent and the utility bills, and had assured us that everything would be okay as long as we paid regularly. We had assumed that there was a mutual understanding between the apartment manager and Edwat regarding the length of time that we were going to stay. Asuqwuo didn't know what questions to ask as it seemed that everything had been arranged. The house was even furnished because Edwat and his ex-wife had lived there, so we didn't need to buy anything while we stayed except food and other basic needs like hygiene and cleaning supplies. It started to feel like we were settling into this transitional home. In my mind, as long as we paid the rent in full, it was a guarantee for us to stay as long as we wanted.

Edwat had gone back to Nigeria with the confidence that we had a roof over our heads, and that we would not have any issues with accommodation. The reverse was actually the case. Apparently, Edwat didn't know the consequences of us living in what was his apartment, even though we were paying the rent.

Our first baptism by fire happened six weeks after Edwat left. It was the last Friday in November and it was (for us newcomers) freezing cold. That night at seven o'clock we picked up Edibenwang from the Taekwondo class that we had enrolled him in. We then rounded out the evening with grocery shopping for the weekend. I was really looking forward to getting home, and we were all hoping to rest and unwind after the week's hullaballoo. I wanted to crash on the couch, lift up my feet, and congratulate myself on surviving another week. I couldn't wait to embrace the warmth in the room. It was not to be.

We arrived home at about nine o'clock and walked along the apartment building corridor toward our door. We were arguing about what meal to prepare for dinner because everyone wanted something different. We got to our door and I turned the key. We were each planning to be the first to get to the couch to relax for a while before starting dinner. The door opened and we were met by empty space. We were just stunned. In unison we gasped out, "Whaaaat!" and then looked at each other in silence. The sitting room was empty— the furniture had all been taken out. At first I thought that someone must have broken into the house, so I panicked and started looking around to see if there were any holes in the walls or windows. I didn't find any.

The pin drop silence continued. Finally, our son said, "Do they burgle homes in Canada?" but since nothing had been broken, the answer was obvious. My husband eventually guessed that someone had come and packed the items out. Slowly we moved from the sitting room to the bedrooms. We went around and checked everywhere. The rooms were completely empty. The bed, the mattresses—everything had been taken out. I was lost for words. I was now thinking about how my child was going to lie on the floor without a blanket. He had never experienced anything close to what we were seeing.

I asked Asuqwuo if he had paid the rent; he answered, "Of course. Yes." A million questions rushed through my mind. Should we go to a hotel? What did we do wrong? Who did this to us and why? Did we offend anyone? Why on earth would someone clear the entire house without informing us? Who did this without any consideration for a nine-year-old child?

My son was now in tears. He had never seen an empty house. He asked, "Mama, where are we going to sleep?" My husband bent his head and wept. I pretended to be the strong woman.

Later that night we discovered the solution to the mystery. Millicent, Edwat's ex-wife, called to inform us that she had come and taken everything. She apologised for not cleaning up afterwards but promised that she would be there the next day to take care of it. We had already cleared up the debris that she left behind, but I didn't tell her that because I thought it would be good for us to meet in person. I could then ask her why she had emptied the house without informing us.

That icy night we slept sitting on the floor. We had searched online to see if any mattress stores were open, but unfortunately none were. We brought out everything from our suitcases to provide warmth and comfort for our son, and we all slept on the floor, wrapped up in bundles of shirts and pants. We were too confused to know what else to do. We stayed half-awake throughout the night; it was difficult to get a good rest as the situation weighed on our minds. I had never slept on a bare floor and neither had I imagined something like this happening to me in the Western world where I thought that everyone was an angel.

The next day was Saturday. First thing in the morning we went out to purchase furniture and mattresses. On our way to the store we called Edwat to narrate the incident. He was shocked as well. Millicent called again later to let us know that she was not able to come now as promised to sweep the house. She explained that she was busy taking care of the children. Out of courtesy, I used the opportunity to ask her if I had done something wrong or if I had offended her. Her response was, "No, not at all." Later that same day her mother called us and told us where we could buy affordable good mattresses and furniture (which by this time we had already purchased). "Thank you for letting us know," I echoed back to her through the phone. End of discussion! No judgement—I didn't know what Millicent's state of mind or circumstances had been to push her into making the decision.

Four weeks later, just when we were getting over the shock of coming home to an empty house, the property manager came to see us. She told us that the lease only had two names on it—Edwat's and his ex-wife's. Our names had never been added. We would have to move out of the apartment. My husband exclaimed, "How come?" He brought out the receipts and showed her all the payments that we had made. She told us that it wasn't about us missing a payment, but about the legal requirements and liability. We had not been added to the lease and could not be added despite the fact that we had evidence of regular payment. The apartment manager continued on by explaining that the only way our names could be added to the lease would be if either Edwat or Millicent came to give their consent. They would have to sign the lease with another witness present. We asked if someone could stand in for Edwat or Millicent, and the property manager said no. She could only allow us to continue living there if the conditions were met. Edwat could not travel from Nigeria to Winnipeg just for the sake of signing a lease agreement and Millicent was too busy taking care of the children to come over. It became apparent to us that we really were going to have to move.

After having slept on the cold floor for one night, we didn't want to risk being thrown out as well, so we set out to find our own home.

During our quest, we met Mercina and her husband (a Nigerian couple) at a community program for newcomers. We chatted with them and shared our story. Right then and there Mercina promised to help, and we exchanged phone numbers. Reaching out and connecting with people outside of my comfort zone had paid off for me. Mercina called the very next day and announced, "I sealed the deal with my apartment manager for you! Come tomorrow at 9 a.m. She is ready, and we are willing to be your guarantors." We arrived at the building and met with the apartment manager who took us on a tour of the apartment. We loved the place. Mercina and her husband co-signed for us, and we moved into our new apartment— the true start of our semi-proper lives.

You may be asking yourself, Why is she telling me this story? I'm sharing it because I learned from this experience. I realize now that if I had done my research before coming, I would have had a better understanding of how to get accommodations. Finding a place for us to live was one of the most important things for me to achieve in a new country. Not being sure of having one had been really troubling for me. When I later shared my experience with a fellow newcomer, she said, "Why didn't you do a search? I took the time to research about Winnipeg, so we got our apartment all arranged before we arrived." In our case, we had depended totally on Edwat.

In the process of time I came to realize that it had not been Edwat's fault. I eventually found out that there are many regulations covering apartment tenancy. Some people may not be able to provide comprehensive information because they themselves are not aware of all the rules. I appreciate now why accommodating us as co-tenants had been so challenging. There had been so many things that I didn't understand then, especially the issue of liability. It simply was not possible for us to live the way we had lived back in our home country. In Nigeria, you can move in with a friend and both of you will have an understanding of how the bills will be shared. The landlord or facility manager will not interfere in your private arrangement. That is why we didn't probe when we had the offer from Edwat.

I now decided that in my new life in Canada I would do research on everything that I wanted to do instead of depending only on what I had heard from people. That would be the case no matter how much trust I had in my sources. This would help me to make the necessary advances to really become one with my new country.

More Progress

All the troubles with accommodation hadn't stopped us from continuing with all the other basic things that we needed to do to become settled. We received our social insurance numbers and health cards in the mail which was a good soother for me and my family.

We were so glad that as permanent residents we were entitled to free health care under Canada's health care system. Universal health care is one of the great benefits of being a Canadian and gives this country an edge over most others in the world.

Opening a bank account was fun. We went to the Royal Bank of Canada (RBC) where we met this very amiable manager who explained the process of opening an account with her bank. She informed us of their newcomer package; it included a credit card with a value of $1,000 to help us with a soft landing. We wanted to reject the offer as it wasn't free and came with interest, but we were advised that it would be a good idea to start building our credit history, so we ended up agreeing to it.

Financial matters were a huge challenge for us as a newcomer family. First, we were faced with the reality of the exchange rate, which drastically reduced the value of the money that we had brought with us. We realised that we had just a one third equivalent in Canadian currency because of the exchange rate. This automatically affected our standard of living. We only purchased the essentials because, in addition to the exchange rate situation, we were still searching for jobs. To be honest, the basics were all we needed anyway: food, transportation, hygiene supplies, and our monthly bills.

One day I was flipping through some paperwork we had received, and I saw an ad with the following: "Neighbourhood Immigrant Settlement Worker. Settlement workers are responsible for providing settlement services to newcomers with permanent residence status for free." Let me use this opportunity to mention Immigration, Refugees and Citizenship Canada (IRCC). This a federal government organisation that is responsible for facilitating the arrival of immigrants. They offer programming to help newcomers settle in Canada. IRCC works through midwife agencies that are located in different parts of the city. These agencies (Family Dynamics is an example) are contracted to respond to the needs of newcomers to the city.

Although English is my first language, I still had delays in accessing services because I didn't know where to get information. We were isolated, with no friends, and we had nobody to provide us with guidance. I immediately checked the contact information in the ad and made a call to schedule an appointment.

On a Wednesday afternoon, we arrived at the settlement workers' office. We were greeted by Fatima and Lee who offered us a seat with a very warm smile. They did an intake for us and helped us find the websites that we needed. They also offered us a box full of groceries and cleaning supplies. We went home and used the websites that they had shown us to download documents; to apply for a family doctor, child benefits, and rent assistance; and also to get tax information.

Picture in Winnipeg, The Canadian Museum for Human Rights.

Later in the week, Lee called me to ask if she could connect me to a Canadian couple, John and Evelyn Watson, who had a reputation for supporting newcomer families in many different ways. I gave her my verbal consent and she shared the couple's phone number with me and vice versa. John and Evelyn in essence adopted us and became our Godparents. I felt a sense of belonging. I felt someone was there for me. A super good feeling came with this encounter. When we met this couple for the first time, Evelyn said, "I don't know how to preach and I don't know how to evangelize; what I can do is support newcomers. I have been supporting new immigrants like this for over ten years." That spoke volumes to me.

Through them, we were able to connect with a church where we began to have fellowship. This helped us in addressing the important issue of spirituality. I volunteered in the church as a Sunday school teacher and assisted in the women's prayer group. My volunteering experience gave me the opportunity to meet so many people who blessed me physically and spiritually. One day I was organizing and preparing right before the women's prayer meeting when the pastor called me out. She prayed for God's blessing for me in a strange land. That was very uplifting for me and it gave me more courage to continue facing the huge challenges of both settling in and navigating the new landscape before us.

Finding My Way Around

We continued to learn more about what it meant to live in Canada. We both wanted to acquire our driver's licence since that would make moving around the city so much easier. Soon after arriving in Canada, Asuqwuo and I did write road knowledge tests as the first step in obtaining our class five licences. The test was multiple-choice and the applicant was allowed to make only four mistakes. The minimum passing score was 80 percent. My husband and I both passed our knowledge tests and he went on to pass his in-car test. However, I failed mine. I did not try doing the in-car test again because I suddenly became very busy.

Driving in Winnipeg is very different from driving in Nigeria. Here, the traffic rules are observed to the letter; that is not usually the case in Nigeria. Traffic hold ups are very limited and manageable here, while in Nigeria the traffic hold ups are regular and sometimes unbearable.

I decided to learn about the bus routes instead. Not that I wouldn't continue to try to get my licence, but I wanted to take it one step at a time. At this time using the bus was more affordable for us than owning a second car. But, as I started patronising the public transit (bus) system, I found that it could be incredibly challenging and sometimes even scary. I really just needed someone who was familiar with the transit system to take me on a one-day bus tour of the whole city. That would have helped me learn how to use the system effectively. But I didn't do that because everyone was too busy and they just didn't have the time to go on a lengthy tour with me. Therefore, I decided that DIY (do it yourself) was the way to go.

On my first day of using the bus system, I planned to take the bus to go drop off my resume. I expected that everything would be the same as it had been in Nigeria. In Nigeria, I had paid cash per trip and hadn't needed a transfer. I didn't know that in Winnipeg paying for a ride covered a trip on only one bus, that a transfer ticket was needed to change buses, and that the transfer must be used within the stipulated time. My first day of using public transit was not fun. I was supposed to use two buses before arriving at my destination. I hopped onto the first bus, inserted the coins, and sat down. I watched everyone. I should have requested a transfer from the bus driver, but I didn't. As we rode along, I took the time to look at every bus stop so that I could get off at the right one. Finally, the bus announced my stop. I noticed that people had been pulling a string when they wanted to get off, so I followed suit and the bus came to a halt at my stop. I got off to catch my second bus, which arrived within two minutes. I hopped in and inserted another fare but still didn't ask for a transfer. I thus ended up paying twice as much as I should have for the trip. As a newcomer every penny counts. When I realised this mistake that had been made due to my ignorance, I felt so bad. "Chai!" as it is said back in Naija (Nigeria). The price of ignorance is truly expensive they often say.

It took me time to understand the bus schedule and the road network in Winnipeg, which was very different from what I was used to. Because of my poor knowledge of geography, it was hard for me to figure out north and south and also hard to figure out the routes even though I understood the road signs. Several times I lost my way. Finding connecting buses was also challenging. In most cases I had to ask for assistance from the driver or a fellow passenger to help me figure out where to stop and catch another bus. I kept pushing on amidst all odds.

One afternoon I met up with a friend who complained to me about how she had been stranded when her transfer expired. She hadn't had any extra coins on her to pay with. She had explained her situation to the driver to see if he could help her. She was very happy when the driver had helped by issuing her a new transfer. After hearing her story, I wanted to make sure that I wasn't put into a similar situation. I decided to look into it and found out that there were different ways of paying for the bus. You could buy regular single-use tickets and ask for a transfer as needed, buy a weekly or monthly pass, or buy a peggo card which could be refilled. I quickly bought a two-week pass and later switched to peggo. With both the bus pass and peggo, I had unlimited travelling hours within the time period that they covered. I began to gain confidence in my understanding of the ticket system and in how bus passes worked. This gave me more freedom in navigating my surroundings and was another step in the settling in process. One step forward, indeed. However, some funny chaps were waiting around the corner for the next lesson!

My Hard Lessons With Scammers

Unfortunately, I soon had some negative experiences that set back my confidence. They had to do with scammers, people who take money from the unwary by tricking them. I am very particular about sharing my experiences because in Canada, "Jackals can walk on two legs and love to take advantage of those unfamiliar and innocent of the procedures." Newcomers like me fall victim in the first years after our arrival because we think we are in paradise. This was exactly my experience. People took advantage of my innocence and my ignorance because I trusted the system and people 100 percent.

One Friday afternoon I had gone for a walk with a friend. I had wanted to start exercising more often as my weight had shot up. As we walked along, we saw a gym and my friend suggested that we go in and make an inquiry. We were greeted by an amiable gym attendant who welcomed us, and we told her that we were there to have a look at their facility and their offerings. "Beautiful," she said, "Welcome to our facility. She took us on a tour, educated us on how to use each of the pieces of equipment, and at the end of the tour asked if I wanted to "sign up." I said yes. She had then given me a form to sign. My understanding had been that she would take my name and that later I would call back and set up my schedule for using the gym. I had thought that I would only start paying after I started using the gym. Two weeks later I got a bill for $2,000. I was shocked. What? I called her and asked why I had received a bill of $2000.

She said, "Oh! You registered as a member."

I said, "No, I only signed up and never used the gym after that."

She said, "It doesn't matter. Signing up means you are a member."

Oh my God! Really! Adopting a curious attitude is one big lesson I have learned. From my experience I learned to ask, "What do you mean?" I knew now that the nuances in Canada were very different from those in Nigeria.

I reported the incident to Amanda and Robyn, my Canadian friends, and they called the gym manager right away. The gentleman on the phone told them the same thing. It didn't matter whether I used the gym or not. My friends and I passed the phone back and forth between us while we tried to reason with him. All parties were now speaking with raised voices. I explained to the manager that I was a newcomer and that I hadn't fully understood what his employee had told me. (Later I realised that this was a common occurrence for both Canadians and newcomers). He told me that he didn't care. "That's part of the price you pay as a newcomer," he said.

I froze. What? No sympathy? In Canada?

My Canadian friends exclaimed, "Unbelievable!" They were shocked and said, "I can't believe this is happening in Canada." They continued, "Eke, if we didn't witness this conversation, we would have thought you exaggerated." They apologized on behalf of Canadians.

My lessons here should have been that this is the price you pay for not being curious, it's the price you pay for putting too much trust in someone, and it's the price you pay for signing documents with poorly understood cost implications. Ignorance was no justification. The people in Canada were just like they were in every other part of the world. I should have realized that I would meet good, bad, and ugly people here. "Bad belle people," those who take advantage of others, "full everywhere" (Nigerian expression for scammers being everywhere). It was a great lesson to learn. However, I apparently still needed another bad experience to really learn it.

This additional experience came in the form of a person who was supposed to be a trusted friend—this time a Nigerian. She showed me a product made by a particular company, and told me that I should buy it. She then said that it would be profitable for me to start selling that product and other products made by the company. I asked her several times if this was a multi-level marketing scheme and she said no. I emphasized that I didn't want to do multi-level marketing. She said, "Oh no, just buy and invite people, you don't have to do anything." It ultimately cost my husband and me $11,000. We learned to avoid those small business opportunities that required initial investments of money—money that we would never reap benefits from. Also, there is a slogan, "Catch them when they newly arrive."

After that experience, we decided to consult with more than five people to make sure that something wasn't a scam. I learned to never give my bank card information or any of our social insurance numbers to anyone when transacting any business. We learned to gather all the information we could beforehand, and to delay signing any document until we knew it was legitimate. I am glad to say that we have not been scammed since, so we moved on to the next stage of our sojourn.

Our First Christmas

We had come to the end of the year and were about to experience our first Christmas season. We found out that in Canada, Christmas was strictly a family affair. It could be very lonely and isolating for a newcomer who didn't have family or friends to visit and share with at this special time of year. In Nigeria, neighbours share meals with you and the streets are bustling with masquerades or street parties. You can literally stay in your house and look outside to be entertained without going to visit anyone. This year, however, our window was half blocked by snow so it was difficult for us to even see outside.

A few days before this first Christmas in Canada, we had nothing prepared. It was just the three of us wondering how Christmas Day would look. We didn't know what to buy and we had only shopped for our groceries.

And then (Oh my God, I can't believe that I am writing this without crying!) John and Evelyn called to let us know that they would be coming to our house. They explained that they would be with family on Christmas Day so they had decided to visit us before that. We were about to learn how to "do" Canadian Christmas! They came to our home for three consecutive days. They helped build a quality Christmas tree for us and they brought us all manner of Christmas gifts. The gifts are too numerous for me to mention them all, but here is a small sample: an air hockey game for our son, pastries, clothes, and perfumes. Their pastor brought us a bouquet of flowers and a microwave as a gift.

On Christmas Day we woke up to find our window completely covered with snow. It was strange, just the three of us in the house, staring at the window, appreciating the wet diamonds reflecting in the sun. But we had more than enough to eat, great Christmas gifts, and thankful hearts for those who had cared about us.

On Boxing Day, Millicent and her mother invited us to dinner at their house, probably as a way to apologize. Who were we to judge? It was uplifting to be invited for a meal by someone we knew. We had a very good meal and chit chat, and were able to bring closure to what had happened at our transitional apartment.

Our first Canadian Christmas was made most memorable by John and Evelyn. Good people are the greatest asset on this journey; when we sought them out, we found them. Finding them helped in the next stage in our development as newbies in a strange land.

My birthday is in January, and on my first one in Canada, the church family—comprising of my pastor John Feakes and his wife and Martins and his wife—hosted us to a sumptuous surprise dinner. That felt really good. I was experiencing the hands of angels. The good experiences started flooding in to erase all the bad ones.

PART 3 | Building A New Life

From A Warm Culture To A Cold One

Because I came from a warm culture, I had assumed that every smile meant friendship and every kindness shown to me meant the beginning of a relationship. I was totally wrong. In Winnipeg, to be precise, kindness is a culture, a way of life. People are willing to provide—you can ask someone a question and they will go all out to help you. But that doesn't mean they will be your friend. You will be provided with free and unconditional support and attention with a smiling face, but trust me—it ends there; there are no strings attached. Though this was initially a shock for me, I learned to enjoy the helpfulness of people in Winnipeg. It really spoke to me about heaven. This is the part that compels me to describe Canada as heaven. Trust me—I benefited from this aspect of Canadians, and I used the opportunity, in a good way, to thrive. I got all the information I could need.

But I did find coming from a warm culture to a cold culture very challenging. Some people saw me as overbearing because of my outward nature, while others admired it. I was always described as overexcited Eke. Because I hug and smile excitedly, I gained myself the new baptismal name of "a hugger." Everyone started describing me as "Eke de hugger."

My son also experienced this difference between cultures.

When we first arrived, he greeted everyone; that is part of our culture. You cannot walk past people without saying hello. One day Edibenwang came back from school and started questioning me about why we greeted everyone in Nigeria. I probed to find out why he was asking. He said that he had observed that people didn't respond to greetings. "They either look at you strangely or pretend they didn't hear you." I advised him to continue greeting people; maybe they hadn't heard him or maybe they hadn't understood his accent. That was a lie; I just didn't want to flog the issue.

I shared my son's experience with a Canadian friend to try to gain a better understanding of what was happening. She said to me, "When someone greets too much we get scared and ask ourselves, What do they want?" She explained that it can be seen as a trap or manipulative.

On the contrary, her husband quickly interrupted and said, "No, that's not so. It's good to say hello." He said that it was civil for people to greet each other. I was confused by getting two different opinions from the same family. Hmmm! The complexity of Canadian culture. Nothing is written in stone. So, I decided to tell my son to go ahead and greet people and that greetings were good. "Keep greeting people even when they don't respond," I said. For myself—I greet and I smile and gradually I win over disciples. One big lesson that I learned from this conversation was to be myself as long as I was not offending anyone. I do what makes me happy. There were many more lessons that I would eventually learn about dealing with cultural differences, and these would help me to guide my son through the new and strange terrain.

Edibenwang

Helping My Child Succeed In Elementary School

As a newcomer parent, I felt vulnerable because I didn't understand the school system in Canada. I had so much fear. Parents who were settled immigrants had brainwashed me with all manner of negative information about the school system and the perceived hate for the black child. I was advised to make sure that my child was perfect in all things. One parent told me that any mistake made by my child would be used against him in the future. She said records were kept forever against black and Indigenous children. As a result of this negative information, I became unconsciously biased against Canadian-born teachers. I saw fault in everything. I interpreted every action as bad, even when they were good. Because I was afraid, I reached out to find information on how to ensure that my child did not become a victim. In my quest to find ways to support Edibenwang, I realised that one of the things that I could do was to be in my child's life as a friend. I could build a stronger relationship with him and engage with him.

I spoke with a couple of newcomer parents both within the school and outside the school on how to make my child strong enough to defend himself. One mother's response was, "Teach him his rights, give him a strong identity, make him proud and confident of who he is, and finally engage him positively so that he gets busy—no time for idle minds." So we set out to register Edibenwang in various extracurricular activities. I told him to share with us every experience that he had in school. This would strengthen our bond and give us the opportunity to provide the needed emotional support. I told him the lesson that my father had taught me when I was only five years old, "Nobody is better than you—there isn't another like you anywhere in the world. So do not allow anyone to put you down in any way. People will always try to put you down but hey, it's about them not you. A good person will always bring out good treasure, but a frustrated person will always want to bring you down. Always remember, it's never about you." I told him that he had to believe that nobody was better than him—this was lesson number one in self-esteem. I repeated these three times.

From conversations with newcomer children, I discovered that they needed as much support as their parents, but unfortunately most of them decried the fact that their parents did not realize how the newcomer children felt in school. Some of the kids told me, "My parents do not know how they laugh at me. They laugh at my food, so I don't open my lunchbox because they say my food smells like rotten potatoes. If I tell my mother, she will not believe me." Newcomer parents often allow their children to figure things out by themselves, not realising that it's not easy for them.

Raising our child in this new and unfamiliar culture was challenging, although thankfully our son was quick to adjust and our approach for supporting him paid off. Speaking and understanding English was not a problem for him and fortunately he made friends with children who were both Canadian-born and new immigrants. I mentioned earlier that one of the reasons that my husband and I had migrated to Canada was to give our child the opportunity to have a pluralistic worldview. To help ensure that our son would achieve this goal, we encouraged these diverse friendships. Things were going pretty well.

In one of the times that I engaged Edibenwang in conversations about his experiences at school, I asked him what he thought the differences were between school in Canada and Nigeria. He said that in Canada the good teachers were really good, and they taught in a friendly way. When I asked about content, he said in most ways it was the same content or even more intense, but the approach to teaching made the content seem easier in Canada. Also, teachers didn't pressure you to do your homework in Canada. You had to be motivated to do your homework; in Nigeria you were afraid of what the teacher would do to you so you were forced to do your homework. Whether motivation or persuasion was used, though, the cost to your education was the same if you didn't do your homework. In Canada however, the teachers are very passive and that is "very deceptive" he said. It was interesting to hear him analyse the situation and to see how quick he was to catch the difference in approach. I told him, "You have to study and do all your homework whether the teacher is smiling or not. What matters is that you have to always do your homework and on time."

I noticed that my son hardly ever accepted or asked for help from us with his homework. He struggled to ensure that he got it right by himself. My son would rather fail and ask for help later than bring questions ahead of time. Edibenwang was proud to learn by making mistakes. He is always proud when he figures things out by himself. One day I forced him to let me help with a particular homework task. I thought I had gotten it right. He told me fearlessly that the method I knew was different from what was taught in his school, and that's why he didn't want me to help him. "Mama, you are not in class with me," he said. I admired his sense of independence. I loved what I was seeing and hearing. He was taking responsibility for his successes and failures and he owned the process. I was thrilled by these positive characteristics that I was seeing in him.

Not everything that Edibenwang told me about his school

was positive. His first bullying experience came when a Canadian-born boy told him that he was not smart. He simply told the boy, "I think you are only telling me who you are; that's definitely not me. I am smarter than you, and I am even the youngest in the class." My son reported the incident to me. I told him that he had done well, but that I would report what had happened to his teacher. When I did, the teacher refused to act. For me, this served to confirm one of the allegations that I had heard about some teachers. I was told that when black children were bullied, some teachers in private schools wouldn't take any action unless the parents of the victimized child were confrontational. (This was definitely not true of all teachers. Some were really good.) Because of the fears that I had developed based on what other parents had told me, I believed that it was because my son was black that the teacher had done nothing. His inaction reinforced my unconscious biases.

When I told his teacher who taught him German what had happened, she reprimanded the other boy in secret and called his mother to tell her about the incident. I was shocked because such cases are often reported to the principal. Anyway, my complaint helped in an unexpected way. That same teacher had been complaining that my son often distracted others in her class. I asked her if he was the only one who was doing this, and she said no. After the bullying incident, she stopped telling me how disruptive my child was. She knew that if she dared to single out my son for disruptive behaviour, then I would remind her of how she had not acted enough in support of my son when another child had harassed him. On another occasion, the students in Edibenwang's class ganged up on him—they all sat on his head! A teacher took me aside later and informed me. I couldn't do anything about it because the person who had disclosed the information wanted to remain anonymous. I didn't report the incident to the principal, and my son didn't want me to do anything either. It was hard for me to keep quiet but I remained voiceless. I felt that my power had been taken from me and that I wasn't standing up for my child. The only thing I could do was to take Edibenwang for an MRI for fear that he had been injured. Fortunately, the results showed that everything was fine. I decided to let it go.

As the school year came to a close, a friend told me that near the end of every school year, the school would set traps for black children so that they could be expelled, especially those in grades six, nine, and twelve. I was also told that the black child had to be super careful because of the tricks used to get them kicked out. She said that Canada was very slippery when it came to black students—especially boys. However, I was starting to be unsure of some of the information that I was receiving because some of the teachers were actually very supportive of my son. In fact, other than the negative incidents that I related earlier, Edibenwang's first year in school was just about perfect, thanks to his homeroom teacher. She had experience working with black children; she understood my son's personality and African culture and was able to guide him through that first difficult period in school. She understood that the Canadian expectations for class behaviour were different from where we had come from, and she did not see him as being intentionally disruptive. She knew that there was no formal class for teaching the code of conduct. Such things as: no touching, hands were to be kept by your side, there was a classroom voice and an outdoor voice, and you didn't shout or yell when in class but you could shout with excitement when you were playing outside—were only learned by the child when they made mistakes during school time.

I do think that this homeroom teacher had an exceptional level of understanding and a highly skilled approach. Overall, though, teachers in private schools in Winnipeg needed a lot of training when it came to diversity and inclusion. It wasn't enough to teach children what was right and wrong plus their reading, writing, and arithmetic. Some of the teachers needed to learn how to accept students from diverse backgrounds;

this was a crucial factor in being able to support them in their education. That is the beauty of diversity. Everyone in leadership positions needs to be practically trained to deal with differences in an empowering way.

As a result of my child's experience, I was forced to ask the principal if they had ever had an African-born child in their school. The principal said that my child was the first. He offered me the opportunity to do a presentation at the school or to connect him with someone who could offer training for the teachers; I saw that as a very good plan. I was glad to see that he was open to my perspective.

The following year, Edibenwang started grade six and he began enjoying his school even more. He made many friends and was now much more familiar with the school system. I had become really rooted in school expectations. I also worked on my biases when I saw more and more that the children were given equal treatment and that the principal was being very patient with me and answering every question that I had. I decided to look at things as they were and no longer from the point of view of the negative stories that I had heard. It dawned on me that I was now on a personal journey of transformation. I was logical and objective in my approach.

Edibenwang's grade six graduation went well; by this point many of his classmates had become close friends. It was all super sweet in the end. Good memories. His teachers gave him an excellent reference letter.

School And Punctuality

Another experience that I had as I tried to support my son in his schooling was related to punctuality. In our culture, being on time was very important. In Nigeria, children were rewarded for arriving at school early. So, we did our best to arrive very early, thinking that it would be good for Edibenwang and for us.

My husband and I had to settle our child first before we could start our daily job hunt. As new immigrants, we wanted to get everything right and leave a good first impression. As the saying goes, you don't get a second chance to create a first impression. We didn't want our son to be late, and we wanted to have the maximum time possible for job hunting.

On one cold and icy morning we arrived at his school at about seven o'clock. We saw the day care supervisor walk in with her child and we followed her, hoping that she was going to let my son into the class. However, she shut the school door behind her. She didn't respond to our greetings, nor did she explain why she hadn't allowed us in. It was -40°C that morning. We rushed back into our car to wait and watch. At eight o'clock we saw the supervisor open the door. By this point other parents had started arriving and we went in together. We dropped off Edibenwang in the day care class and went on our way.

This pattern of being shut out continued for several days. We didn't understand the reason behind the supervisor's actions, and we were not bold enough to ask. Plus, we were the only ones there at that time, so there was no one else to ask.

We were confused. What was going on? Was it because we were black? The answer of course was no, but to be honest, I thought that she was acting in a racist way because of all the negative stories that I had heard. Eventually, we had to remove our son from the day care and strategize on how best to get him to school by eight o'clock so that we could start our job search. We started scheduling our appointments for nine o'clock instead.

Several months later I became bold enough to start asking questions. I had made friends with some Canadian parents and teachers by this point and one day I started telling them about my experiences. One of the ladies burst out laughing. She said, "It's because of liability."

I asked, "Liability for what?"

She explained about the issue of insurance, the hours it covered, and why the school authority or day care supervisor couldn't allow any child into the building earlier than the approved time. I thought Really? You must be kidding me. This was the second time that we had come up against the issue of liability, the first of course being when we had been forced to leave our transitional apartment. We were finding out the hard way that in Canada it was very important to precisely follow systems and processes.

"Why didn't she explain why she was locking us out?" I questioned.

The woman said, "You didn't ask, and she may have assumed that you just wanted to dump your child and run off. Plus, in Canada, we keep to our bubble unless someone steps out and asks. It is also possible that she may have thought that you didn't speak English and that she wouldn't have been able to communicate with you."

Oh, really? I could literally have been left outside in the freezing temperatures to die. What if we had not brought our car? This was different from where I came from. Someone would nicely (or even by yelling) have told us not to come too early because of policy. The message would definitely have gotten through.

I felt like this situation was an example of the cold culture in Canada and how the culture encouraged people to stay within their bubble. On the other hand, the warm culture in most African countries encouraged people to be more outgoing. Perhaps this difference in cultural practices and their interpretations was the cause of many misunderstandings between newcomers and Canadians. Newcomers do not necessarily make mistakes, but they may lack the confidence to step up and ask questions because of their fear of being misunderstood. Their Canadian counterpart may not want to overstep certain boundaries and thus they do nothing to help. The results for us were by no means catastrophic, but I saw how they might have been for some.

Middle School And High School

My son's first middle school was a mixed bag, and he ultimately moved to another school because we had switched homes.

The new school was challenging for many reasons. First off he was simply coping with being a budding teenager and the higher-than-previous expectations. My son blew it one day when he joked inappropriately with a young man who then reported him to the vice principal. When I was called to a meeting about the issue, I made the mistake of blaming my child in front of the vice principal. I should have kept quiet and dealt with the issue at home.

Guess what happened to my son on his graduation day from middle school? After congratulating my child, the vice principal had tactfully reminded him of the mistake that he had made three years earlier. "You have really grown to be a distinguished and dependable young man," he said. "I still remember when your mum yelled at you in my office."

Really? In a Christian school! Was this a joke? Maybe for him yes but for me No with a capital N. Where I had come from, you didn't remind children of their wrongs especially when they had been forgiven.

Like every story there were good parts and bad parts. There were lots of good memories from Edibenwang's middle school years that were very soothing. To be able to see those good things clearly, I had to keep confronting my own biases.

I met white Canadian teachers who were exceptionally kind and polite to my son. His music teacher facilitated his enrollment in the Winnipeg Boys Choir. He noticed that my son was a good singer and Edibenwang became one of the 150 children who performed in Ottawa during Canada's 150-year anniversary celebrations. We are grateful to his music teacher who was able to see his talents.

After middle school, he transferred to a high school located closer to our new home. He graduated with honours and is now in university. Somehow, we had jumped over the hurdles and gotten through the rough patches while learning more about our new country. The journey was still on, and we cheered ourselves along the way.

What We Did Well

It is very important to newcomer parents to find out as much as they can about their child's new school. They need help with this, just like any newcomer needs help in any number of different ways. My husband and I took the time to read the school policies and that helped us. Through the school, we became friends with older, settled parents who had more experience with the school system. This was also a big help. I became confident in asking questions! Through these channels, I learned that it was important as a newcomer parent to enrol my child in day cares within the school system; this allowed me the time to go job hunting and to do the other countless things that I needed to do, to function as a Canadian. In addition, I made time to volunteer in my child's school. I interacted with my child's teachers to learn more about them, and to allow them to learn about me as well. Participating in my son's school activities was very helpful.

Ensuring cultural balance was another challenge that I faced with my child. It is very easy for immigrant children to become assimilated and to lose their heritage. In the beginning, I saw my son struggling to maintain this cultural balance. Sometimes on his way back from school he would be very quiet and I would notice him gazing into space. I

First fishing activities as a family taken when we went to visit Kenora.

would interrupt his thoughts and try to probe into his world. Sometimes I succeeded and made him speak out. At other times I'd pray with him and try to reassure him that all would be well.

Over the years, I have come to realise that immigrant children walk around wearing two hats and they fight the same fight as their parents. But because they don't know how to present it to their parents, their fight is internal. This is especially true when they know that their parents are struggling as well. At school my child tried to be Canadian and at home he struggled to keep fitting in with our cultural heritage. That was hard for him. I tried to help him understand the differences between the two cultures and why he had to wear both hats. I tried to promote my culture at home but to be sensitive to certain practices in Canada that were

Going for a boat ride on our first family vacation at Kenora with Canadian friends.

different from those in Nigeria. I worked hard to provide my son with the needed cultural support by constantly reminding him that he was a Nigerian and by providing him with information that was good for him at that particular time. As a result, he was able to affect a balance between the two cultures. He developed the necessary skills to navigate his way through the two systems in which he found himself: He was a Nigerian when he was with Nigerians. And he was able to function in his new very polite Canadian terrain. This helped me in turn to focus on my own journey.

My Employment Journey

Job Hunting

We had now settled our child in school, and I was feeling much better about my ability to navigate some of the Canadian systems. Because I now had a reasonable idea of how things worked, I felt really confident at the beginning of my search to find gainful employment. I didn't realise that I had a long way to go. It turned out to be a long journey of mental and physical Shock.

In Canada, jobs are not hanging on trees to be harvested—you search for them. When it comes to job hunting, different people have different experiences and approaches. In general, though, newcomers start first with a job unrelated to their training (what is sometimes called a survival job), and then only later plan on how to step into their dream job. This is because they have to settle their bills which start coming in as soon as they arrive. That was what my husband did; slowly, through reinventing his career path and getting additional education, he was able to move to where he is today. Unfortunately, most people are literally forced to give up the pursuit of their dream jobs because of the frustrations involved. Newcomers who are educated, speak English, and formerly had great and well-paying careers back home, find it frustrating that they can't find the same job here in Canada upon arrival.

Typically, employers prefer applicants who have Canadian work experience. Certifications outside of Canada usually don't count until you do certificate recognition, which costs a lot of money (no matter how much we wished that they didn't). That's why it's not uncommon for a taxi driver to have formerly been an accomplished educator, engineer, or doctor in their home country. Sometimes when jobs are offered in your field it's only an entry level position, because employers don't think that you can handle all the workplace requirements.

Newcomers like me can easily fall prey to discrimination and exploitation in the workplace. Some employers recognize the sense of urgency and desperation among us to secure jobs, so they will have us take lower wages than desirable and even give us dangerous roles, not to mention long hours. For many, this is where we get our first shock and, in some cases, depression starts to creep in.

I was very determined, and I didn't let my dreams die. I believe everything is possible. When I was job hunting, people would often tell me to take any offer (after all it was the money that was important), but I searched for a job with a purpose. I didn't allow myself to be distracted. I stayed focused.

There are so many barriers affecting newcomers—obstacles that keep them from being employed in their dream job. They include language, age, family, certification, and access to information. I once talked with a lady who told me, "I was a lion in my country, but here I became a cat."

"Why is that?" I was curious.

She explained, "It will take me years to achieve my dream because I don't speak English. I have to learn English. That will take a long time, and I will be getting older and older." To encourage her, I told her the story of a ninety-five-year-old immigrant woman whom I had met and talked with. She had been a medical doctor back in her home country and her medical studies had been in her first language. The lady told me that she came to Canada at the age of forty-seven with no English and three toddlers. She said that she had started as a cleaner in a hospital so that she could be in a medical environment. She enrolled in English classes and eventually was accepted into a program that allowed her to earn a medical degree in Canada. She practiced as a medical doctor in Canada for over twenty years. She lived her dream. Yes, it took time—but she did it.

I broke my own barriers through self-determination. I asked questions, looked for people with shared experiences, became vulnerable as a story teller, I kept sharing my own experiences with others, and asked for help. I saw myself as a child (and still do) so that I could learn and adapt when necessary.

I came to Canada thinking that I would have a job handed to me on a silver platter; I had worked with a Canadian organization back in Nigeria, I had an impressive resume, and I spoke English. I was a black, educated, confident woman with what I thought were very good credentials. Canada is a gender sensitive country, and I felt very sure that I was positioned to attract a job that I needed. The reverse was the case.

Right from the start of my honest job search, my otherness became obvious. I was reminded several times that I had an accent. What accent? Since I spoke British English, I thought that I had been speaking normally—until I was told that I had an accent. Really? I have an accent? I was also told that my English was different from how Canadians spoke. I kept asking, "What does that mean?" Nobody could give me an explanation until one day when I went to a coffee shop. The service was slow, so out of concern I asked the employee, "Are you alone?" She didn't seem to understand what I meant. We kept going back and forth asking the same questions until another customer said, "She is asking, 'Are you by yourself?'" Really? What was the difference? In the context of the situation, "By yourself" meant "alone" to me, but to the employee, my "alone" had meant that she was single. Really. Interesting! What was the difference?

In order to learn to speak using the Canadian descriptive style, I actively participated in "typical Canadian events." I gained a love for the Canadian way of expressing ideas. It is very subtle: words like would, should, and could are mainstreamed into sentences. I became used to using these words and I enjoyed it. It made me feel relaxed when I was using them. These words express humanness and each time that I didn't hear them, I felt like something was missing. Good for me!

I continued to work on my language skills so that I was able to code switch when needed, and I kept up my job search. Even though I thought I was making progress, the feedback I got told me something different. Each time I came face to face with any employer I would hear: "Oh! Work on your tone, it is harsh." "You don't have Canadian experience." Or, "You need to understand Canadian workplace behavior."

I wasn't deterred. I continued to build my community by connecting and networking. This played a very important role in my job search. And, it produced results. Through my network, I was offered my first contract job in Canada based on the recommendation of a Canadian-Nigerian colleague from One Sky. I was invited to be a keynote speaker on "Perspectives of Solidarity: Dialogue about Solidarity in International Development" for students who had graduated from the University of British Columbia in Vancouver. My airplane ticket and honorarium were all paid. It was a very good sign for me and ushered in hope and confidence.

After my trip to Vancouver, I continued my job search and also started volunteering at several organizations to learn how to communicate in the Canadian way. I then felt prepared for my dream job, which was working in a lead position in an international development agency, much like I had done in Nigeria.

Along the way, I heard a lot of myths and discouraging things. A friend told me that I could only get a job if I had my driver's licence. He said that all the jobs that I could be offered would require me to move around the city. I asked if there were no jobs that required me to stay in the office or use a bus to move around? He said, "Not for newcomers. You will spend at least five years before getting such a job."

"Big lie!" I told him. "I will get a job without my driver's licence and I will perform exceptionally well. Just watch me!"

He had laughed boisterously and said, "I really love your confidence, Eke."

In my quest for a job I went to an African store. Luckily, I met a Nigerian man who directed me toward Manitoba Start, a non-profit organization that helps new arrivals find their place in the local workforce.

Both Asuqwuo and I connected with Manitoba Start and also with Altered Minds Inc. (another organization supporting new immigrants). They did an intake for us at their offices, and our information and orientation sessions were scheduled. At Manitoba Start, we spent two weeks receiving information and undergoing orientation. These sessions were very intensive but rewarding. The training gave us an idea of what the local employment market looked like; it was a good class. After the sessions with Manitoba Start, we went to Altered Minds for more information and training. There, I remember one of the facilitators said to us, "This information is overwhelming. I suggest you keep the handouts, you will have need to refer to these resources as you continue your settlement journey. It may not be useful today, but it will be in the future." We took her advice and that's exactly what happened. The experience and knowledge that we gained from the training proved to be very useful to us, especially since we didn't have anyone to give us reliable guidance.

After two weeks of orientation with the Manitoba Start program, my husband had three job offers. One was outside of Winnipeg but he didn't want to leave the city, the second was as a career coach which lasted for only four weeks, and the last one was in the health sector.

My journey was longer. I sent out seventy resumes without getting a single invitation for an interview. That led to lots of frustration.

Volunteer

Another newcomer referred me to an agency called the Success Skills Centre, which specializes in helping people with higher university degrees find jobs. There I met my career coaches, Ha and Alka. I spent two weeks in training at the centre, and I attended follow-up sessions over the following six months. During those months I was a serial volunteer. I volunteered with the Charis Centre (part of Manitoba's Union Gospel Mission), the Immigrant and Refugee Community Organization of Manitoba, and the Winnipeg School Division.

When I was volunteering at the school division, I was told that the Family Dynamics organization was looking for a volunteer who would help facilitate a program for newcomer women. I ended up meeting with Salem, who worked for Family Dynamics as the newcomer settlement worker for the Tuxedo area in Winnipeg. She shared the position expectations with me and asked me if I was interested— adding that after this volunteer commitment ended, I would get a reference letter. I accepted.

As a volunteer for Family Dynamics, I was responsible for facilitating a driving program for immigrant women whose first language was not English. It was the funniest experience of my life because I didn't drive; I had to study the Manitoba Public Insurance Driver's Handbook and then use a simulator to train the newcomer women who wanted to go for an in-car road test.

When I was in the process of facilitating the driving information session, Salem, the employee who supervised me, told me about a job opening with Family Dynamics. I read the job posting and realized that I possessed the skill set, experience, and competencies needed for the position.

When I came to the end of my six months of training and volunteering, I sent out three resumes (including one to Family Dynamics) and all three organizations invited me for an interview. Finally! I ended up with three job offers and all three were related to what I had been doing back home. I had to choose—it was a great feeling. I chose Family Dynamics because I was going to be working with newcomers, and so I felt that the organization itself would be patient with me as a newcomer. Also, the job would give me the space to grow and interact with different types of people.

I started as a neighbourhood immigrant settlement worker and I eventually became a program coordinator for the Community Settlement Program. The settlement worker position was related to my field, but it was not exactly what I had done before. However, I was sure that I could transfer my skills and experience because they appeared to fit well in terms of the job responsibilities. I stepped into that first job thinking that I would be leaving after one year because it was only a one year term position. Fortunately, after that year, it turned out that the same position came up in the same organization, just at a different location. The new position was full time permanent.

Some job offers come in disguised form; one cannot predict what comes up after you get your foot in the door.

Adjusting To My Workplace

As I mentioned, jobs are not harvested from trees, even though that is how Canada is promoted to immigrants. I had to look for a job, and it took me some time before I was "a fit." Though getting my dream job was a struggle, keeping it and growing in my career was even more challenging. It was here that I battled other people's unconscious bias, passive-aggressive remarks, microaggression, lack of standard respect for one another, and behavioural double standards. I experienced "dehumanizing engagements" in meetings and "dismissive microaggression" launched in emails. On several occasions, my authentic nature was belittled. I looked at these actions as discrimination because I saw myself being treated badly and differently from others simply because I was seen as being ambitious. Some blacks were the worst; they ganged up to try to slow my progress, and passed on provocative insinuations to like minded colleagues who fell for their cheap lies. This is when I started to realise that the smiles that I had seen at work might not be what they had originally seemed to be.

It's at this point where most educated immigrants like me start having mental health issues because we expect to be trusted by our very own. But like the old adage goes, "The rat in the house is the one who takes the bush rat on a tour around the home so that they know where the food is stored." Another wise saying from the Bible is, "A man's worst enemy will be members of his own household" (Matthew 10:36). With this knowledge, I was more prepared to face the attacks from some people of the black race who hid behind the effect of colonization in order to perpetuate evil against each other.

I have had to endure all of this for the sake of making progress. Through it all, I have realised that the discrimination that I faced and still face is a symptom of people finding a difference between themselves and someone else, and then treating the other person in a negative way because of that difference. People are people, whether black, white, red, or any other colour of the rainbow, and we are all capable of this negative behaviour in response to any number of differences. The complexity of human beings cuts across race and it doesn't matter where you run to. You will have to fight these demons in people.

I was a black woman who sought promotion, worked hard, had great ideas, and was opinionated, and I was labeled by most people, including my black folk, as being ambitious or aggressive. Why I was discriminated against by my fellow blacks was what I didn't understand. It made me realize that even those who I considered to be part of my "group" could try to pull me down. I was expected to be meek and humble. My transparency was offensive to many people. One person described me as having a "voice of authority" as though that was a bad thing. There are so many potential labels out there that can be discouraging or make you doubt yourself.

At one point, a lady that I worked with (a contract staff) and who was my friend decided to stand against me for no reason. This lady had been very good to me before that. We had worked together for a long time. She had been very supportive of me and to be honest she had taught me all that I needed to know about the childcare policy. After I had been working for 2 years, she started whispering lies about me, stating that I had not been following policy and guidelines in implementing programs. This was an example of someone who was trying to bring me down so that I would be fired. My friend, who was Canadian born, decided to send a petition to my head office, the implication being that she had obtained authentic proof of the allegations. (Let me quickly state here that my experience in Canada is that some people prefer to report you directly to your supervisor at the slightest mistake that you make. They do this rather than first talking to you about the problem. We had called that evil in Nigeria. At my workplace in Nigeria, we had confronted our offender before taking the problem to our supervisor.)

Unfortunately for my very wonderful friend, whom I still love, her supposed witness and ally denied ever having told her anything. She said to my friend, "I don't understand English very well. (me no English) I'm sorry you thought I said something bad about Eke." But it came too late. I was already facing mediation by this point. Later, the newcomer told me that I had spoken to her in an unfriendly tone and that she suspected I was operating with double standards (Nepotism). This was why she had approached my co-worker to embellish her story because she didn't know how to approach me. The result of the complaint was that, through mediation, my Canadian co-worker and I had to set up rules for our relationship. As well, I had to take extra steps to make sure that I always followed due process in relation to some policy and I became more sensitive especially to those who struggle with speaking English. I did my best to adhere to the conditions that were set out in this mediated outcome.

I had never experienced mediation before, and because of it I learned many things. I look back now and I am very proud of the skills and knowledge that I gained from the process. I also found out what a single but dangerous story could do. The contract staff didn't obtain the result that she had wanted (or maybe she did). Maybe she had wanted me to learn and improve—which is exactly what I did.

One of my Canadians friends, Amanda, would repeatedly tell me that you couldn't make 100 percent of the people like you, but if you scored 80 percent, it was a passing grade. She told me to stay focused on what I wanted to achieve. In my first year of partnering with her she sent me a card that read, "I love working with you." Another Canadian friend who was a school principal invited me to her office and said, "Don't let your voice die, use it like Maya Angelou. Keep inspiring people. You are very inspiring, Eke. You have great skills in pulling people together": what a soothing comment in the midst of storms. These and many more positive comments from friends motivated me to continue being me. The support from them and from others too numerous to mention gave me the strength to push on.

The more I experienced these mixed negative and positive reactions, the more I realised that it didn't matter where I was or in which country I was living in—I just had to be prepared to encounter both the good side and the bad side of people. It was like my father had told me and I had told my son: it was about other people and not me; I had to be more determined than ever to just be myself. This was one of my reasons for writing this book.

The more labels people had placed on me, the more I realised how important my own voice was. I was a threat to people who had a complex, but I was also much appreciated by people from many different races. Again, this was a display of human complexity. Sometimes, in two identical situations, I would be belittled by people in one case and in the other case receive praise. This was true for all the Canadians and blacks that I called friends or acquaintances. The more I became aware of my own excellence, the more it helped me to know that something about me was special. Inasmuch as I was conscious of the culture of my new country, I had to stop it from swallowing my identity. The good and the bad comments from people forced me to quickly learn—and understand—the rules of engagement in the workplace. I needed to use these rules to succeed not only at work, but also in my life outside of work. I learned to deal with people according to their personalities, rather than by complaining about them.

Because of this mélange, I decided not to change the core of who I saw myself to be. I continued to be true to myself. I made sure that I performed well and actually knew what I claimed to know; when I didn't know, I admitted it and asked for help. As was said back home in Nigeria, "He who asks questions does not miss the road." I had almost forgotten this vital rule in life. This was even better than keeping quiet and pretending I know so I keep asking for help. I continued interacting with people who would challenge me to build my skills and competencies. I associated with people who had something to offer me, I intentionally chose those that I wanted to relate to, and I didn't let mockers discourage me. I remained focused on my tasks, performed excellently, and did my work. I became more flexible and adaptable; this was important—I was dealing with others who had complex natures and who reacted in various ways to those who saw things differently from them.

Before I moved to another level in my job, I faced many false allegations. People mocked me. Somebody told me, "This isn't Africa where you can expect to be appreciated or promoted based on hard work. Here nobody rewards hard work." That person went so far as to tell me that getting more education (which I wanted to do to prepare myself for career advancement) didn't matter—you just stayed in your position and grew on the job. "What?" I whispered silently to myself. This comment came as a shock. Then there was another surprise—a few months later I found out that the same person was taking a course to upgrade. Another "bad belle" person (evil person). They are everywhere.

I have not changed my values regarding work. On my career journey, four things have always mattered to me: integrity, authenticity, excellence, and truth. I still work with the same attitude that I had back in my home country, and it is paying off. Whenever I have to work extra hours to complete my task, I do. One morning my manager walked into my office and she said, "I am here to say thank you for all you have done. I just want to let you know that I acknowledge your extra hours and all your effort. You have done well!" What is more important than having your efforts be acknowledged by your supervisor. My manager is not a person who plays with words; she means what she says so I knew that she was truly happy with my efforts.

This experience increased my resilience and resourcefulness. It proved to me that what is good is good no matter where you are or who you are; I made up my mind to adapt to different working practices as long as it was for good. Over the years, I learned to contribute to small talk while still maintaining my boundaries. I mind my own business at work and focus more on succeeding and fulfilling my contractual agreement. This, and my basic Nigerian-ness have helped me to grow in all aspects of my new Canadian identity.

Growing In My Career

After I had been working at Family Dynamics for a year, I had a conversation with a friend regarding wages and salaries. She brought out a salary scale and explained to me how people were graded in Canada. I made up my mind to upgrade by studying for a second master's degree. Through this, I experienced schooling in Canada and I gained a better understanding of how universities work here. This has helped me to support my child while he is in university, plus I now have a Canadian degree to show when needed.

For me, higher education in Winnipeg was a different ball game altogether. Reflections and case studies were core practice. The 11:59 p.m. syndrome became a song in our mouth. All assignments had to be handed in by this time or you would start losing marks by the minute. And trust me, it was not a joke.

To succeed academically and otherwise, I had to put in my best effort. They were very challenging times because I was juggling full time work, school, and family. How else could I upgrade myself, though, if I was desiring to get to the next level of my career? In my home country I had upgraded my position after two years, and now, for psychological reasons and based on the information that I had received, I wanted to move to the next level in my Canadian career. I wanted to have the feeling that I was now close to doing the job that I had been doing back home, even if it wasn't exactly the same.

Surprisingly, rather than appreciating what I was trying to do, some people started throwing darts at me. These "bad belle" folk don't give up, do they? That expression from Nigeria helped me to disregard the bad comments: "Oh! She is ambitious." "Oh, I don't know what she is rushing for!" Or, "You mean that 'superwoman?'"

But also, I had great minds telling me: "That is the way to go girl!" Or "Go for it!" So many of my Canadian friends and also my former (now late) supervisor supported me in every way. The few people who stood by me were genuine and worked with me all the way through.

Some people said, "Oh, you work too hard!"

"What does that mean?" I asked. Their "working hard," to me actually meant "working smart" because I now had results to show for my perseverance and determination. I had my job and I now had an additional certificate.

So, whose reality counted, theirs or mine? Who determined what hard work was? What were their parameters and what were mine? Those were some of my internal thoughts that helped me to process the situation; they also strengthened my self-determination. I focused on my work—on whatever would help me to make a positive impact.

One of the experiences that was shared with me by a fellow black lady was very inspiring. Her story became my mantra. It was all about how she had moved up the corporate ladder to become a manager. She came to Canada as a young, vibrant student, and after graduating she got a job with an agency. Her supervisor was always giving her extra tasks and she made sure that she completed them; this was in addition to her regular responsibilities. The other teammates would gossip about her, saying that she was a dumping ground for her supervisor. She ignored them and continued with her work. She said, "Eke, do you know that even my black sisters mocked me and said to me, 'These people will use you and dump you.'"

She told me that she hadn't argued with them, but instead had said to them, "Yes, I can be used and dumped on, but the skills and experience will be with me forever. Nobody can take that away from me. I am also learning for the future." She said that this was her regular reply each time they came up with discouraging comments. She had remained focused.

Looking to the future with faith by grace.

She went on to tell me, "My sister, those 'out of the box' tasks exposed me to new knowledge and ideas, and gave me a bigger network and community. My skills were sharpened, and new ones were built." She told me that the best part of her story had happened when her supervisor had wanted to go on vacation. Management had asked her supervisor if she had someone on her team that could take her role and fill in for her when she was away. Her supervisor had not blinked an eye before recommending my friend, and my friend had then acted in that capacity for three months.

On her supervisor's return, my friend had automatically been moved into that role as her supervisor had suddenly been promoted to another higher position. My friend acted in that capacity for two years before—based on the strong recommendations of that same supervisor—she was poached by another organization. And my friend finally said to me, "Eke, it paid off. Those skills and experiences are the same ones that I am using in my current position." Working strategically could be interpreted as hard work by others, but what matters is what you yourself name it.

My friend's story reminded me of what my father had always told me: "Follow your bliss my daughter, and the rest will fall into place." And I was doing just that. I was following my passion for my profession by working hard to attain my dream job. I believe that there is always a reward for me for whatever I do; it's a divine principle whether in Canada or Africa. It's the habit of finding good in every experience and turning happenstance into great nuggets of value.

PART 4 | How I Deal With Adversity

How I Deal With Adversity

Canada is a highly educated country of readers where you will find a significant amount of research relating to equality, diversity, and inclusion. You can easily find studies on rights, colonization, racism, gender, equality, privilege, and much more. Should you care to know or learn about societal vices, there is a lot of knowledge about them that is freely shared. Awareness is very high. This has its advantages and disadvantages.

Racism, passive aggression, lateral violence, colonization, integration, and assimilation are words that you hear often in professional settings and training sessions. Most agencies and organisations have written policies to address racism and discrimination. However, this is not always a guarantee that they do not still exist.

For me, the issue was how to deal with others' microaggressions. These would manifest as dismissive and dehumanising words; exclusion from meetings; or being labelled as angry, loud, imposing, or intimidating.

In the beginning it was hard for me. I was really frustrated and depressed because I fought against these stereotypes and they kept affecting me.

I felt that I was experiencing racism and lateral violence ("anger taken out on people in marginalized groups by other people who are also in marginalized groups"). To deal with what I was going through, I took the time to reflect on my own and others' actions toward other people. I accepted that some people saw me as loud and strong. I compared what I was experiencing here with behaviours that I had experienced in Nigeria. I also observed what was happening around me and I sought out other people's stories. I came to the conclusion that the conflicts that I was experiencing here also happened back home. I realised that what I was seeing as racism was actually wickedness painted in a different color. Otherwise, how would I explain it when I saw a white Canadian being mean to a fellow white person? I had even seen a white person hate a fellow white person unto the person's death. I said to myself that I would have called it racism if they had tried to do that to me. In my home country, I had experienced hate as well as kindness from my own people; I had been defended by someone who I had considered to be an enemy and I had been betrayed by someone who had pretended to be my friend.

One day in my second year as a settlement worker, I visited my head office and ran into my executive director in the corridor. She asked me, "How is it going with your job?" I suddenly broke down and started sobbing. When I looked up, I noticed tears rolling down her cheeks. My Executive Director was weeping with me. I told her in between sobs that it was hard out there. She replied, "I know it." It was a soothing experience to have a white woman weep with me; it had come at a time when I felt like the people who saw me as different were against me. I am sure that she soon forgot this moment, but it spoke volumes to me.

I had heard about racism so frequently that I was now interpreting many things through that lens. This incident motivated me to stop being so determined to see things that way. What I am trying to say is that I recognized that discrimination and exclusion—not based on race—did exist in my home country and I overcame them. Why then should I have allowed myself to be swallowed by these things in Canada—whether they were based on race or not? I didn't arrive at these thoughts in one day; it took some time. I still knew that there was systemic racism, but I had to help myself to avoid frustration and improve my mental health.

One of the reasons why I had been distraught in the beginning was because I had had such high expectations of Canadian people and the Canadian system. I had almost literally thought that I was going to heaven. But people are complex; we cannot predict their behaviour. Sound mental health requires me to become deaf and blind to all the ideologies that others use to interpret my experiences. Instead of going along with someone else's perspective, I have learned to prepare myself to fight with a positive attitude; the law of the spirit is to overcome evil with good. I try to stay positive no matter the situation.

Holding Onto My Spirituality And Identity

In dealing with these experiences, I decided to focus on being rooted in my higher emotions and to connect with my spiritualty. My Bible tells me that, ". . . for whatever a person sows, this he will also reap." (Gal. 6:7b New American Standard Version) The Bible also says, "The heart is deceitful above all things,

And desperately wicked; Who can know it?" (Jer. 17:9 New King James Version) and it goes further to say, "A good man out of the good treasure of his heart bringeth forth that which is good; and an evil man out of the evil treasure of his heart bringeth forth that which is evil: for of the abundance of the heart his mouth speaketh." (Luke 6:45 King James Version) You can see why my mantra in Canada is: Whatever you do is all about you—not me—as long as I am doing my best.

Through it all, I continued to root myself. To be honest, sometimes there were situations that really broke me down, but I quickly remembered to change the game by connecting with my higher being, love, and forgiveness, and by allowing the higher power to defend me. And that worked. I stopped engaging in frivolous arguments and I stopped trying to prove myself.

Eventually, I made up my mind to embrace my stereotype. My stereotype formed my identity and as such was a strong weapon of defence for me. I loved people calling me a black woman, aggressive, and loud. I was Black and I loved all the labels. There was so much good in me and I didn't care what someone else's opinion was. I heard comments about myself that I had never heard before (or maybe I had but now they were making more of an impression on me because I hadn't expected to hear them in Canada). As an immigrant, I never forgot my identity and spirituality. These two were my main weapons.

One of my courses in university had been about self-determination, and stress had been placed on the importance of identity. The knowledge that I gained from this course helped me to hold my head high. Instead of feeling like a dummy in meetings, I now felt that I should be heard in a good way. This was especially true when others made contributions that I didn't agree with and nobody made a mockery of them. So why couldn't I make my contribution? It would be better for me to make mistakes and learn from them, than to keep quiet and die because I was Black. I am a confident Black Woman from Nigeria, and I have successfully passed this self-confidence on to my son.

Don't think that I have forgotten the essential values like respect, integrity, excellence, and being authentic. These qualities will always make me stand out no matter who is trying to run me down. My former supervisor once told me, "We are not stupid." I had asked her what she meant. She had replied, "We know who is who." Isn't that sweet to the ears! Standing out without compromising and being spiritually rooted in integrity has protected me on this journey and has helped me to see the silver lining in the clouds that I have encountered along the way.

I Have Come A Long Way

It was 2016. I was still new, was seeking knowledge from every corner available, and was making use of every opportunity around. Roselyn Advincula, former coordinator for settlement workers, signed me up for some workplace training. Roselyn has been very supportive on this journey as well. In my early work years, she would sign me up for training opportunities. This time she signed me up for a training about starting a conversation with new immigrants whose first language was not English. The training was focused on engaging newcomers using familiar images to start up a conversation in different settings. As the training had progressed, I hadn't been quite appreciating the importance of the topic. It wasn't making sense to me; it seemed a waste of time. But I remained calm and didn't judge; I waited patiently to see the end of the matter.

As the training had continued, I noticed that people were becoming very excited, were glued to what the instructor was saying, and were very focused on the material. Then it dawned on me that this was a very important skill for me to have and the course a golden opportunity to start to learn it. With this realization, I asked a Canadian-born lady who was sitting next to me what her perspective was on how long it would take for a newcomer to settle. By settling, I meant that

Taken at Times Square New York when we went for vacation.

the newcomer would understand and navigate the system with confidence; do well academically and spiritually; be mentally, emotionally, and financially grounded; be on an established career path; and finally breathe and beat their chest with some level of confidence before ultimately declaring, "I am home and settled!" She had replied, "If you are the smart type, it will take you at least ten years before you can begin to be sure of what you are doing. This includes understanding the cultural nuances, and building confidence. Then you can begin to thrive."

In another development session, I had asked my supervisor, "At what point do you say 'I know how to work with Canadians?' " She had said, "Canada is a mosaic so there is no one size fits all answer. You must follow the river as far as it flows, adjust to suit the situation, and be open to everything but not attached to anything; this will help your mental health." I applied both principles and I am here to say it is working. Come October 2023, it will be ten years since we came to Canada. Looking back, I feel that I am stronger.

In 2022 it suddenly dawned on me that what my Canadian coworkers had told me all those years ago was right. There was no one size fits all answer.

Counting My Blessings

On this journey I have experienced countless blessings from many different people, races, and tribes. I cannot help but mention them in this book.

Many of the people who have played key, positive roles in my journey are teachers, principals of schools, church community, friends, colleagues and politicians, though I won't be able to mention all of their names. These people gave me strength and a voice. They were people who helped me to stand strong as I started my journey as a new immigrant and a settlement worker.

Carol(late), Amanda, Tonya, Alka, Ha, Roselyn and Salem were my first career connections. They stood up for me in my personal and career life. They advocated for me when I needed an advocate. They helped me integrate into my role as Settlement worker. They championed humanity through their actions and encouraging words.

In schools, Caterina, Troy, Patricia, Marla, other principals and English as an additional language (EAL) teachers and independent consultants and contractors; Nesreen, Margerit, Grace and Julie who served in my agency had all been there for me and they had helped me to succeed in my career.

My professors in school. I can't stop mentioning my dear Tabitha who was my guardian angel. Claire, Jennifer, and Tamara provided me with insight on how to navigate the school system. Racheal, Hanock, Temobi, and Chelsea my four go-to classmates. And host of others in my department too numerous to mention their names

My past and present supervisors contributed to my success in different ways when they provided mentorship and given honest feedback. They are both very direct in providing feedback: they could either tell me that certain things were not right, or their countenance would change which clearly told me when I needed to change my strategy. I love their style because it is very Nigerian. My colleagues at the Pembina office helped and supported me in different ways too numerous to recount. Not forgetting my South Winnipeg community members like Sharon who will help mobilise resources for newcomers.

The church community, African community and Nigerians supported me spiritually and physically; when I experienced loss, they were there to comfort me.

Undeniably, my family has been my first support system. Very thankful to my son Valour and Francis my husband who are always the first to experience my sadness and my joy- strong shoulders for me to lean on.

I am very grateful that some people tried to pull me down; these difficult situations turned out to be blessings in disguise. I became better through the experiences in managing people who are difficult. I became a guru in managing people using their personality. My pain became my gain.

Relationship building is key for me and belonging to multiple communities helped me. It allowed me to grow and opened up new opportunities.

People are my greatest asset, but I had needed to choose whom I wanted to hang out with. It had been much like choosing a good book to read.

To Suguren (God) be all the glory, for great things he has done for me and my family. Great is HIS faithfulness. Amen!

Resting My Case

Over the past nine years of journeying into building a life in Canada, I have learned that settlement is a personal journey. With resilience and self-determination, I believe that everything is possible. I have used every challenge as a stepping-stone.

I recognise that there are many battles yet to fight—settling in a new country is not easy.

I have come to appreciate the fact that understanding my socialization and my cultural behaviours is important so that I can improve and have a challenging but rewarding settlement experience.

Along my journey, I have come to realize that newcomers experience very difficult transitions. Mutual understanding of this fact by both newcomers and Canadians could go a long way toward both developing a healthy transition process and establishing a system that would form a strong bridge between Canadians and new immigrants.

I would like to suggest that settled Canadians learn about newcomers, because newcomers are already learning about Canada. I think if we learn more about each other, it would go a long way toward erasing the prejudices that I think are rooted in misunderstandings and misinformation on both sides. I would suggest that newcomers water down their expectations of Canada and know that life here is as hard as it is back home, but in a different way.

One day when I was on the bus, I heard a guy speaking in a very loud voice, "All of you new immigrants have come here because of money—to make money, take our jobs, and ruin our country." Yes, to make money and to get jobs, but to ruin the country? No! Just as has been happening for centuries, newcomers and immigrants like me have come to contribute knowledge to our new country. I and my fellow newcomers have come to make it count!

I have not regretted migrating to Canada. Why? Because I have the quiet life I have always desired, a life where I can make progress at my own pace. The reason I am writing this book is simple: my expectations were far beyond the reality, so I was not prepared. I would have felt differently if I had migrated to America. I would have been mentally prepared to fight. But when I heard Canada, I heard Heaven. Settlement in my opinion is what we call a "wicked problem." A wicked problem is a development term that "defines problems that are impossible or near impossible to solve. To even attempt to solve them, a collaborative effort is essential." It would be wonderful if everyone could work together to make Canada a true Paradise in spirit as well as in truth.

In spite of all my experiences I believe Canada is a great country. For me, this country is a marriage of beauty and opportunity spiced with freedom and liberty.

Indeed, it has been a journey of dying and being resurrected so that I can make it to heaven. Truly, in our situation, Canada has become our heaven and we have died and are still dying—not a physical death, but rather some of our perceptions and ideas are dying and have died; new ones are sprouting each day. Trust me, the journey to our Canadian Heaven is closer than when we first began.

www.ingramcontent.com/pod-product-compliance
Lightning Source LLC
Chambersburg PA
CBHW071213120626
46546CB00006B/2537